a new translation

by Ben Waggoner

Troth Publications
2017

Published by The Troth
325 Chestnut Street, Suite 800
Philadelphia, Pennsylvania 19106
http://www.thetroth.org/

ISBN-13: 978-1-941136-13-3 (paperback); 978-1-941136-14-0 (e-book)

Cover image: Figurine from Lindby, Skåne, Sweden; courtesy of Swedish Historical Museum (CC BY 2.5 SE)

Troth logo designed by Kveldulf Gundarsson, drawn by 13 Labs, Chicago, Illinois

Cover design: Ben Waggoner

Typeset in Garamond 18/14/12/11/10

dedicated to Gus Gissing

orð mér af orði   orðs leitaði,
verk mér af verki   verks leitaði

INTRODUCTION

Hávamál, "Speech of the High One," survives in a unique medieval Icelandic manuscript known as the *Codex Regius*, copied around 1270 from an earlier manuscript. Together with the other poems in the *Codex*, as well as a few from other manuscripts, *Hávamál* is part of a collection usually known as the *Poetic Edda*. Ten of these thirty-one poems tell stories of the Norse gods, often using them as frames to present lists of lore, names, or advice. The rest tell the cycles of legends of the heroes Helgi and Sigurd.

The *Hávamál* as we have it may have been assembled from several earlier poems.[1] The opening section, sometimes called "The Gnomic Poem", gives practical advice on how to survive and prosper in a society where personal reputation is paramount, political and legal wrangles are inseparable from daily life, and hospitality to guests is a high virtue, yet friendly behavior might cover up sinister intentions. The poem describes how to conduct oneself, as a guest and as a host; how to handle alcoholic drinks; how to win favor among men; how to treat friends and enemies; and how to handle wealth.

At stanza 90 the talk turns to advice in love; this section is sometimes called "The Poem of Sexual Intrigue." The speaker blames women for being deceitful, but admits that men are no better. He tells about an unsuccessful love tryst—and finally identifies himself: he is the god Odin. Then we hear of a more successful amorous adventure, in which Odin wins the precious mead of poetry, which gives poetic inspiration to all who taste it. This myth is told in more detail in Snorri Sturluson's *Edda*, and is frequently alluded to in other poems.

In the next section, the *Loddfáfnismál* or "Loddfafir's Words", voices in Odin's hall begin giving advice to someone named Loddfafnir. These verses echo the more practical advice already given—but the voices begin to mention *rúnar*, runes. The word could mean the letters used to write various Germanic languages before the adoption of the Latin alphabet; but it could also mean "secrets" of various kinds, and exactly which meaning is intended is sometimes left ambiguous. The poem reaches its climax as Odin tells Loddfafnir how he won knowledge of the runes through an act of self-sacrifice, and then, in what is sometimes called the *Ljóðatal* or "List of Songs", lists eighteen magic spells that he has mastered. Although he does not explain how the spells are actually cast, both carving runes and chanting spells are mentioned. Thus despite its patchwork origins, the poem progresses fairly steadily from plain and practical advice to myths and esoteric matters.

Hávamál has been translated into English at least twelve times. Why do we need yet another one?

Translation is like performing music. Each translator, like a performer of a classic, brings his or her own tastes and experience to the piece. Each translation, like each performance, brings out different aspects of the original work, and the performer must balance what the author intended (which is not always clear) with what "works" for him or her. A great symphony may have been performed many times—and yet still invite new performances that plumb new depths in the music. Translation is like that; no matter how many times a classic like the *Iliad* or the Bible or the *Edda* has "already been done", there are always new aspects of the work to seek out and try to reveal. The existing translations all have their strengths. All the same, I felt that I could still find something new in this endlessly fascinating poem.[2]

I based my translation on Guðni Jónsson's normalized text, but I have also consulted the Íslenzk Fornrit edition, as well as every English translation I could get. I haven't tried to duplicate the alliteration and rhythm of the original Norse exactly. I've let words alliterate, and I've kept the stress pattern, when I felt I could do so without disrupting the flow of words or betraying the meaning.

I send my heartfelt thanks to Michaela Macha for her wise editorial counsel. All remaining errors are entirely my own.

HÁVAMÁL

1. Before a man takes one step forward,
he should look around,
he should spy around
all doorways—because it's hard to be sure
where enemies await him on a bench.

2. Hail the givers! A guest has come in;
where shall this man sit?
The man who's had to sit on the stack of firewood[3]
is quite keen to try his luck.

3. A man who's come inside needs fire,
when chilled up to his knees;
a man who's traveled over the mountain
has need of food and clothes.

4. A man who comes to a meal needs water,
a towel, and a friendly welcome,
good manners (if he might get them for himself),
talk, and silence in turn.[4]

5. A man who travels widely needs wits—
everything's easy to handle at home.
A man who doesn't know anything,
but who sits with the wise, gets winked at.

6. A man must not be boastful about his own wisdom,
but guard his wits, instead.
When a wise and discreet man comes to a homestead,
there is seldom woe for the wary,
for a man never gets a more steadfast friend
than plenty of common sense.

7. The wary guest who comes to a meal
keeps silent and sharpens his hearing;
he listens with his ears, and looks around with his eyes;
thus every wise man searches his surroundings.

8. Lucky is he who has won for himself
praise and words of support—
but what the man has inside another's heart
is more difficult to deal with.[5]

9. Lucky is he who gets praise and good sense
for himself, as long as he lives,
for a man has often taken poor advice
from another man's heart.

10. A man bears no better burden on the road
than plenty of common sense.
It seems better than wealth, in an unfamiliar place—
such a thing is support for a poor man.[6]

11. A man bears no better burden on the road
than plenty of common sense.
He carries no worse provisions in open country
than too much ale to drink.

12. Ale is not as good as they say it is
for the sons of mankind,
because the man who drinks more, understands less
how to keep control of himself.[7]

13. The bird that loiters over drinking bouts
is called the heron of forgetfulness[8];
it steals the minds of men.
I was fettered with this bird's feathers
in Gunnlod's courtyard.[9]

14. I became drunk, I became overly drunk,
at wise Fjalar's home.[10]
A drinking bout is best when each man
recovers his own wits.

15. A chieftain's child should be silent and attentive,
and be bold in battle;
every man should be glad and cheerful,
until he meets his own death.

16. A cowardly man thinks that he'll live forever
if he steers clear of fighting;
but old age will grant him no truce,
even if spears grant it to him.

17. A fool gawks, when he comes on a friendly visit;
he mutters to himself, or shuts up.
All at once, if he gets a drink,
the man's mind is exposed.

18. Only he who journeys far and wide,
and has traveled much,
knows what sort of mind every man commands;
he's got good sense.[11]

19. A man must not cling to a cup,[12]
but let him drink mead in moderation;
let him speak usefully or be silent.
No man will blame you for bad manners,
should you go to bed early.

20. A greedy man—unless he keeps control—
eats a lifetime of grief for himself;
a foolish man's belly often causes laughter
when he comes among the wise.

21. The herds know when they should head for home,
and then they leave the grass;
but an unwise man never knows
the measure of his own belly.

22. A wretched man of mean character
jeers at everything.
He doesn't know what he'd need to know:
that he's hardly flawless himself.

23. An unwise man stays awake all night
and ponders all sorts of things.
Then he's worn out when morning comes—
and everything's still wrong, as it was.

24. An unwise man thinks that all those
who laugh along with him are his friends;
he doesn't even realize it if they're slandering him,
if he sits among the wise ones.

25. An unwise man thinks that all those
who laugh along with him are friends;
then he finds out, when he comes to the Thing,
that he has few men who will speak for him.

26. An unwise man thinks that he knows everything,
if he has a hiding place in a corner;
he doesn't even know how to respond
if people put him to the test.

27. An unwise man who comes among people—
it is best that he stay silent;
no one knows that he knows nothing,
unless he talks too much.
A man who knows nothing doesn't even realize
that he's talking too much.

28. He who knows how to ask, and how to respond
in the same way, seems wise.
Sons of men can conceal nothing
of what is said[13] about a man.

29. A man who never shuts up speaks
quite enough worthless words;
a fast-talking tongue, unless it has restraints,
often summons up evil for itself.

30. A man should not mockingly wink at another,
though he's come to a friendly gathering;
many a man is thought to be wise, if he isn't questioned,
and he gets to sit quietly, keeping his skin dry.[14]

31. He who slips away seems to be wise,
when a guest is mocking a guest;[15]
he who mocks at a meal doesn't know for sure
if he's chatting with enemies.

32. Many men are true to each other,
but they quarrel at a meal.
That strife will forever exist among men:
a guest is hostile to a guest.

33. A man should often take meals early,
unless he's come on a friendly visit.
He sits and looks around hungrily, acts famished,
and can't ask about many things.

34. It's a twisting path to a poor friend,
even though he may live on the high road;
but straight roads lead to a good friend,
even though he may have travelled far.

35. He should go—a guest should not always
stay in the same place.
A beloved man becomes loathed, if he sits
for too long on another's benches.

36. A house is better, though it may be small;
everyone's a hero at home.
Though a man may have two goats and a hut thatched
    with twigs,
that is still better than begging.

37. A house is better, though it may be small;
everyone's a hero at home.
Bloodied is the heart of the man who must beg
for his food at every meal.

38. A man must not walk one step away
from his own weapons on the field,
because it's hard to be sure when a man might have need
of a spear, out on the road.

39. I haven't found a generous man, nor one so kind
    with his food,
that something in return wouldn't be accepted;
nor one so free[16] with his own wealth
that repayment would be hated, if he were to take it.

40. A man should not put up with losing money
which he has received as his own.
Often he saves for hated ones what he meant for loved
    ones;
many things go worse than he expects.

41. Friends should cheer each other with weapons and
    clothing;
that may be seen on themselves.[17]
Those who repay gifts and give again stay friends the longest,
if the friendship continues to go well.

42. A man should be a friend to his own friend
and give a gift for a gift;
men should receive laughter for laughter,
but lying for lies.

43. To his own friend, a man should be a friend—
to him, and to his friend's friend;
but no man should be a friend
of his own friend's enemy.

44. You know, if you have a friend whom you trust well,
and you want to get good from him,
you must mingle your thoughts with his, and share gifts;
go to meet him often.

45. If you have another man whom you mistrust,
yet you want to get good from him,
you must speak fine words to him, but think deceitfully
and repay lying with a lie.

46. Also, concerning the man whom you mistrust,
and you have doubts about his intentions:
you must laugh with him and speak falsely;
what you give should match what you get.

47. Once I was young, I traveled alone,
then I got lost on the roads;
I felt wealthy when I found another:
a man is a man's joy.[18]

48. Generous and brave men live best,
they seldom nurse sorrow;
but a cowardly man fears everything,
and a stingy man is always troubled by gifts.[19]

49. In a field, I gave my clothes
to two wooden idols;[20]
they looked like warriors when they wore clothes—
a naked man is shamed.

50. A fir tree that stands on a farm[21] withers;
neither bark nor needles protect it.
The man whom no one loves is like that;
how is he to live long?

51. The love between bad friends blazes,
hotter than flames, for five days;
but then it dies down when the sixth day comes,
and all the friendship takes a turn for the worse.

52. One should not give a man only large gifts;
often one earns praise with little.
With half a loaf and a cup poured out,[22]
I gained comrades[23] for myself.

53. On little sands, on little seas,
the minds of men are small.
So all men haven't grown equally wise;
mankind is a mixed bag.[24]

54. Each man should be modestly wise;
may he never be too wise;
living is finest for those men
who know just enough about many things.[25]

55. Each man should be modestly wise;
may he never be too wise,
because a wise man's heart seldom grows cheerful,
if the one who has it is completely wise.

56. Each man should be modestly wise;
may he never be too wise.
A man should not know his fate beforehand—
his mind is most carefree.

57. A log catches fire from a log, until it's burned up,
a flame is kindled from a flame;
a man grows wise in his words from a man,
but grows dull from being conceited.[26]

58. The one who wants to have another's wealth
or life must arise early;
a wolf lying down seldom gets a joint of meat,
nor does a sleeping man gain victory.[27]

59. He who has few laborers must get up early
and go see about his own work.
Many things hinder the man who sleeps all morning;
keen men have already won half their reward.

60. Dry firewood, bark for thatching a roof—
a man knows just the right amount
of wood that may last him
for a season and a half-year.

61. A man should ride to the Thing washed and well fed,
though he not be clothed too well;
let no one be ashamed of his shoes and breeches,
nor of his horse, though he not have a good one.

62. An eagle snaps and stretches his neck
when he comes to the ocean, the ancient sea;
such is a man who comes among the crowd
and has few men who will speak for him.

63. Every knowledgeable one must ask and answer
if he wants to be called wise;
one man must know, not a second one;
all the folk know, if there are three.[28]

64. Each of the wise counsellors should keep
his own authority within limits;
then he who comes among bold men finds
that no one is keenest of all.

65. [Watchful and heedful should every man be,
and wary of trusting in friends.][29]
For the words which a man says to others,
he often gets paid back.[30]

66. Much too early I came to many places,
but too late to some;
the ale was drunk, or some wasn't brewed;
one who's loathed seldom finds just the right occasion.[31]

67. Here and there I would be invited home,
if I didn't need food at mealtime,
or if I were to hang up two hams[32] at the home of a true
    friend,
where I had eaten one.

68. Fire is best among the sons of men,
and the sight of the sun;
his own health, if a man can have it,
and living without a fault.

69. A man is not entirely ruined, though he be in ill
       health;[33]
one man is blessed through sons,
one through kinfolk, one through plenty of wealth,
one is well-blessed[34] through deeds.

70. It is better for a living person than for a non-living
       person;
a living man always gets a cow;
I saw fire blaze up before a wealthy man,
but outside, a dead man was before the doors.[35]

71. A lame man rides a horse, a handless man drives a
       herd,
a deaf man fights effectively;
a blind man is better than a burned one would be;
no one has use for a corpse.

72. A son is better, even though born late,
after his father has passed;
memorial stones seldom stand near a road,
unless kinsman raises them for kinsman.

73. Two will defeat one. Tongue is head's bane.
I expect a hand hidden under every fur coat.

74. He who's sure of his provisions is glad when night
       falls.
Ships' yardarms are short.
An autumn night is changeable;
there are many kinds of weather in five days,
but even more in a month.[36]

75. The one who knows nothing does not know[37]
that money makes a fool of many a man.
One man is wealthy, another not wealthy;
one should not blame him for misfortunes.

76. Cattle die, relatives die,
you yourself die likewise;
but glorious reputation never dies
for anyone who gets a good one for himself.

77. Cattle die, relatives die,
you yourself die likewise;
I know one thing that never dies:
the judgment over each dead one.

78. I saw full livestock pens for Fitjung's sons;[38]
now they bear a beggar's staff.
Such is wealth, like a wink of an eye;
it is the most unreliable of friends.

79. If an unwise man manages to gain for himself
wealth or pleasure with a woman,
pride grows in him, but never common sense;
he marches straight ahead into folly.

80. It's tested and proved, when[39] you ask the runes—
those that come from the Advisers,[40]
those which the Primal Advisers made,
and the Mighty Speaker[41] colored—
he is best off, if he stays silent.[42]

81. One should praise the day at evening, a woman when
    burned,[43]
a sword when tested, a maid when married,
ice when one crosses it, ale when drunk.

82. In wind one should chop wood, in fair weather row
    out to sea;
in darkness chat with girls—many are the eyes of day;
one should use a ship for sailing, but a shield for
    protection,
a sword for a blow, but a maiden for kisses.

83. One should drink ale by the fire, but skate on ice;[44]
buy a thin horse, but a dirty blade;
fatten up the horse at home, but set the dog free to
    scavenge.[45]

84. No one should trust in the words of a maiden,
nor that which a woman says,
because hearts were shaped for them on a turning
    wheel,[46]
fickleness laid in their breasts.

85. A breaking bow, burning flames,
a gaping wolf, a cawing crow, [47]
a squealing swine, a rootless tree,
a rising wave, a boiling kettle,

86. a flying arrow, a breaking wave,[48]
one night's ice, a coiled serpent,
a bride's pillow talk or a broken sword,
a bear's play or a king's child,

87. a sick calf, a willful thrall,
a seeress's pleasing speech,[49] freshly killed warriors—

88. (early-sown fields let no man trust,
nor too early in a son;
weather rules the fields, but wit rules the son;
either of them is risky)—

89. his own brother's bane (though he meet him on the
   road),
a house half-burned, a swift horse—
a steed is useless if one leg is broken—
may a man not grow so trusting that he trusts in all
   these.[50]

90. Such is the love of women, of the ones who think
   falsely:
as if one were driving a steed on slippery ice, without
   spiked horseshoes—
a frisky two-year-old, and poorly tamed—
or as if he were to handle a ship in a furious breeze with
   no rudder;
or as if a lame man had to catch a reindeer on a thawing
   mountain slope.

91. Now I speak openly, because I know both;
the mind of men is deceptive to women;
when we speak most finely, we think most falsely;
that deceives sensible minds.

92. He who wants to win a lady's love
must speak fine words and offer wealth,
praise the body of the bright girl;
he who woos will win.[51]

93. No man should ever reproach another
for falling in love;
lust-kindling looks often catch a wise man
but don't catch a fool.

94. A man should not blame another for anything
that happens to many men;
the mighty desire makes the sons of men
fools where they once were wise.

95. The mind only knows what is close to the heart;
a man is alone with his thoughts.
No sickness is worse to every wise man
than to take contentment in nothing.

96. I found that to be true when I sat in the reeds
and waited for my beloved.
The wise maid was flesh and soul to me;
all the same, I didn't have her.

97. I found Billing's wife[52] in bed,
the sun-bright girl was sleeping;
the joys of high station seemed nothing to me
unless I might live beside that body.

98. "You must come again in the evening, Odin,
if you want to speak of your love;
everything's lost, unless only we know
of such lust together."

99. I turned and left, and thought that I was sure
of winning love and delight;
This is what I thought: that I would have
all her heart and pleasure.

100. When I came next in the night,
the entire warband was awake,
with blazing lights and torches held high—
the path to failure lay before me.

101. Again, near morning, when I had come again,
the household had gone to sleep—
then I found a bitch, tied onto the bed
by that lovely woman.[53]

102. Many a fine lady, if one gets to know her fully,
is fickle towards a man;
I found that true, when I tried to lure
the wise woman into deceit;
the shrewd girl sought every humiliation for me,
and I had nothing from her.

103. At home a man should be merry,
cheerful to guests, and shrewd,
mindful and well-spoken, if he wants to be well-
        informed;
often he shall gain good things.
He who can't say much is called a big blockhead;
that's the nature of a stupid man.

104. I met the old giant, now I have returned;
I accomplished little by keeping silent.
I spoke many words to my advantage
in the halls of Suttung.[54]

105. Gunnlod gave me, on the golden seat,
a drink of the precious mead;
I left a poor repayment behind for her,
for her full affection,
for her heavy heart.

106. I let Rati's point make room for me
and gnaw through the stone;[55]
above and below me were giants' paths,
thus did I risk my own head.

107. I made use of my precious shapeshifting skill;[56]
few things are lacking for the wise,
for Odroerir is now brought up
to the temple of man's protector.[57]

108. I am doubtful that I would have come back,
out of the courts of the giants,
if I hadn't used Gunnlod, the good woman,
over whom I laid my arms.

109. The next day, the frost-giants came
to ask the High One's counsel
in the High One's hall;
they asked about Bolverk—[58]
had he gone with the Gods,
or had Suttung slain him?

110. I believe Odin has sworn an oath on the ring;
how can his word be trusted?
He had Suttung tricked out of his drink,
and made Gunnlod weep.

111. It is time to whisper on the thyle's seat
at the Well of Wyrd;
I watched and was silent, I watched and considered,
I heard the speech of men;
I heard them speak of runes, nor were they silent in
    giving counsel
at the High One's hall,
in the High One's hall,
I heard them speak thus:

112. I advise you, Loddfafnir,[59] to take this counsel—
you'll profit from it, if you learn it,
you'll get good from it, if you take it—
don't get up in the night except to look for news,
or to look for a place to "do your business."

113. I advise you, Loddfafnir, to take this counsel—
you'll profit from it, if you learn it,
you'll get good from it, if you take it—
you must never sleep in the arms of a sorceress
so that she enfolds you in her limbs.

114. She will arrange it so that you pay no attention
to the Thing, nor to the chieftain's words;
you won't want food or fun with others;
you'll go to sleep full of sorrow.

115. I advise you, Loddfafnir, to take this counsel—
you'll profit from it, if you learn it,
you'll get good from it, if you take it—
never seduce another man's wife
to share secrets[60] with you.

116. I advise you, Loddfafnir, to take this counsel—
you'll profit from it, if you learn it,
you'll get good from it, if you take it—
if you feel the urge to travel on mountains or fjords,
provision yourself well with food.

117. I advise you, Loddfafnir, to take this counsel—
you'll profit from it, if you learn it,
you'll get good from it, if you take it—
never let a wicked man know
that misfortune's befallen you,
because you'll never be rewarded with any good wishes
coming from a wicked man.

118. I saw a man wounded from above
by the words of a wicked woman;
a deceitful tongue was the death of him,
and the charges were untrue.

119. I advise you, Loddfafnir, that you take this
        counsel—
you'll profit from it, if you learn it,
you'll get good from it, if you take it—
you know, if you have a friend whom you trust well,
go and meet him often,
for the road that no one treads is overgrown
with brushwood and tall grass.

120. I advise you, Loddfafnir, that you take this
        counsel—
you'll profit from it, if you learn it,
you'll get good from it, if you take it—
attract a good man with friendly words[61]
and learn healing spells, while you're alive.

121. I advise you, Loddfafnir, that you take this
     counsel—
you'll profit from it, if you learn it,
you'll get good from it, if you take it—
you must never be the first
to abandon your friend;
sorrow devours your heart, if you can't speak
all your mind to one person.

122. I advise you, Loddfafnir, that you take this
     counsel—
you'll profit from it, if you learn it,
you'll get good from it, if you take it—
you must never exchange words
with stupid apes,

123. because you will never be repaid
for good deeds by a wicked man,
but a good man can ensure
that you'll receive praise.

124. Whoever decides to speak all his mind to someone
shares kinship with him.
Anything is better than being false;
he who only speaks pleasant words is no friend to
     others.

125. I advise you, Loddfafnir, that you take this
     counsel—
you'll profit from it, if you learn it,
you'll get good from it, if you take it—
you must not bandy three words with a worse man;
often the better man fails
when the worse man wins.

126. I advise you, Loddfafnir, that you take this
    counsel—
you'll profit from it, if you learn it,
you'll get good from it, if you take it—
don't be a shoemaker or an arrowsmith,
unless you do it just for yourself;
if the shoe is badly made, or the arrow is bent,
curses will be called down on you.

127. I advise you, Loddfafnir, that you take this
    counsel—
you'll profit from it, if you learn it,
you'll get good from it, if you take it—
wherever you recognize evil, call it evil,[62]
and give no peace to your enemies.

128. I advise you, Loddfafnir, that you take this
    counsel—
you'll profit from it, if you learn it,
you'll get good from it, if you take it—
never rejoice in evil,
but let yourself be pleased with good.

129. I advise you, Loddfafnir, that you take this
    counsel—
you'll profit from it, if you learn it,
you'll get good from it, if you take it—
you must never look upwards in battle—
the sons of men grow mad with terror—
lest warriors bewitch you.

130. I advise you, Loddfafnir, that you take this
        counsel—
you'll profit from it, if you learn it,
you'll get good from it, if you take it—
if you want pleasant dealings with a good woman
and to get treated well for doing it,
you must make fair promises and keep them;
no one grows weary of good, if he gets it.

131. I advise you, Loddfafnir, that you take this
        counsel—
you'll profit from it, if you learn it,
you'll get good from it, if you take it—
I ask you to be cautious, but not too cautious.
Be most wary of ale, and of another man's wife,
and of a third thing: that thieves make a fool of you.

132. I advise you, Loddfafnir, that you take this
        counsel—
you'll profit from it, if you learn it,
you'll get good from it, if you take it—
never hold up a guest or a wanderer
to laughter or scorn.

133. Often those who sit inside don't clearly know
what sort of people have arrived;
there's no man so good that he doesn't have a flaw,
nor one so bad that he's good for nothing.

134. I advise you, Loddfafnir, that you take this
    counsel—
you'll profit from it, if you learn it,
you'll get good from it, if you take it—
never laugh at a grey-haired speaker;
often what old men say is good;
often sensible words come from shriveled bags
that hang among the hides
and swing among the skins
and trail among the tatters.[63]

135. I advise you, Loddfafnir, that you take this
    counsel—
you'll profit from it, if you learn it,
you'll get good from it, if you take it—
don't sneer at a guest, or shove him out the door;
treat the wretched well.

136. Strong is the door-beam that must swing
open to everyone;
give rings, or else guests will wish
every harm to befall your limbs.[64]

137. I advise you, Loddfafnir, that you take this
    counsel—
you'll profit from it, if you learn it,
you'll get good from it, if you take it—
when you drink ale, choose the power of the earth,
for earth counters ale-drinking. [Fire counters illness,
oak counters straining, an ear of grain counters sorcery,
the elder-tree counters strife at home—you must invoke
    the moon for hatred—
earthworms counter bites, but runes counter evil,
the earth shall counteract a flood.][65]

138. I know that I hung on the wind-blown tree
all of nine nights,
spear-wounded and given to Odin,
myself to myself,
on that tree, of which none knows
from where the roots run.

139. They did not refresh me with a loaf, or a horn of
drink—
I looked down, I took up the runes,
screaming I took them, I fell back from there.

140. Nine great songs I learned from the famed son
of Bolthorn, Bestla's father,[66]
and I got a drink of the most precious mead;
I was sprinkled with Odroerir.[67]

141. Then I began to grow fruitful and be wise
and grow tall and thrive,
one word after another called for a word from me,
one work after another called for a work from me.

142. You will find runes and interpreted letters,
very great letters,
very strong letters,
which the Mighty Speaker colored
and the Primal Advisers made
and Hropt carved among the Advisers.

143. Odin among the Gods, Dain for the alfs,
also Dvalin for the dwarves,
Asvid for giants,
I myself carved some.

144. Do you know how you must carve? Do you know
   how you must read?
Do you know how you must color? Do you know how
   you must test?
Do you know how you must ask? Do you know how you
   must offer?
Do you know how you must slaughter? Do you know
   how you must sacrifice?

145. It's better not to ask than to offer too much,
a gift always looks for repayment;
it's better not to slaughter than to sacrifice too much.
Thus Thund[68] carved before the dawn of the folk;
he rose up where he returned.

146. I know those songs which no ruler's wife knows,
nor any son of man.
One is called "help"; it will help you
against accusations and sorrows
and absolutely all sufferings.

147. I know the second, which the sons of men need
who want to live as healers.

148. I know the third: if I have great need
to restrain men who hate me,
I blunt the blades of my adversaries;
their weapons and staffs don't cut me.

149. I know the fourth: if men bring bonds
to fetter me hand and foot,
I chant, so that I can walk:
the fetter breaks from my legs,
the bonds from my arms.

150. I know the fifth: if I see a spear
flung into the ranks with malice,
it cannot fly with such force that I cannot stop it
if I catch sight of it.

151. I know the sixth: if a warrior wounds me
on the roots of a strong tree,[69]
and the man pronounces hatred for me—
the harm devours him, rather than me.

152. I know the seventh: if I see leaping flames
on a hall, around the benchmates,
it cannot burn so much that I cannot save it;
I know how to chant that spell.

153. I know the eighth, which is beneficial
for everyone to learn:
where hatred grows among princes,
I can quickly settle it.

154. I know the ninth: if the need arises
to save my ship on the water,
I calm the wind upon the waves
and send all the sea to sleep.

155. I know the tenth: if I see fence-riders[70]
sporting up in the air,
I make them leave, losing the way
back to their own forms,
back to their own minds.

156. I know the eleventh: if I must lead
long-time friends to battle,
I chant beneath the shield,[71] and they will travel in might,
safely to war,
safely from war,
safely they come away from there.

157. I know the twelfth: if I see a hanged corpse
swinging upon a tree,
I carve runes and color them,
so that the man walks
and talks with me.

158. I know the thirteenth: if I should throw water
on a young warrior,[72]
he will not fall even if he enters a battle;
the hero will not sink before spears.

159. I know the fourteenth: if I must tell of the gods
before a host of men,
I know the details of all the gods and alfs;
few unwise men have this knowledge.

160. I know the fifteenth, which the dwarf Thjodrerir
chanted before Delling's doors;
he chanted strength for the gods, success for the alfs,
deep thought for Hroptatyr.[73]

161. I know the sixteenth: if I want to have all
of a shrewd girl's love and pleasure,
I turn the thoughts of the white-armed lady,
and twist all her mind about.

162. I know the seventeenth: so that the young maid
will hardly steal away from me.
You will lack this song, Loddfafnir,
for a long time,
although it would be good for you, could you get it,
useful, could you learn it,
needful, could you acquire it.

163. I know the eighteenth, which I never teach
to a maiden or to a man's wife—
everything is better if only one knows;
that follows the end of the songs—
except for the one alone who embraces me,
or else who is my sister.

164. Now the High One's words are spoken in the High
    One's hall,
most needful for sons of men, useless to sons of giants.
Hail to him who spoke them! Hail to him who knows
    them!
May he who learned them use them! Hail to those who
    heard them!

TEXT AND TRANSLATIONS:

Auden, W. H. and Paul B. Taylor. *Norse Poems*. London: Athlone Press, 1981.

Bellows, Henry Adams. *The Poetic Edda*. Princeton, N.J.: Princeton University Press, 1936.

Bray, Olive. *The Elder or Poetic Edda, Commonly Known as Sæmund's Edda. Part I: The Mythological Poems*. London: Viking Society for Northern Research, 1908.

Chisholm, James. *The Eddas: The Keys to the Mysteries of the North*. Houston: Illuminati Books, 2005. http://www.woodharrow.com/images/ChisholmEdda.pdf

Crawford, Jackson. *The Poetic Edda: Stories of the Norse Gods and Heroes*. Indianapolis: Hackett, 2015.

Dodds, Jeramy. *The Poetic Edda*. Toronto: Coach House, 2005.

Dronke, Ursula. *The Poetic Edda. Volume III: Mythological Poems II*. Oxford: Oxford University Press, 2011.

Guðni Jónsson. *Eddukvæði*. Akureyri: Íslendingasagna-útgáfan, 1954.

Jónas Kristjánsson and Vésteinn Ólason, eds. *Eddukvæði.* Vol. 1. Íslenzk Fornrit. Reykjavík: Hið Íslenzka Fornritafélag, 2014.

Hollander, Lee M. *The Poetic Edda.* 2nd ed. Austin: University of Texas Press, 1962.

Larrington, Carolyne. *The Poetic Edda.* Oxford: Oxford University Press, 1996.

Orchard, Andy. *The Elder Edda: A Book of Viking Lore.* London: Penguin, 2011.

Terry, Patricia. *Poems of the Elder Edda.* Philadelphia: University of Pennsylvania Press, 1990.

OTHER SOURCES:

Adam of Bremen (transl. Francis J. Tschan). *History of the Archbishops of Hamburg-Bremen.* New York: Columbia University Press, 2002.

de Vries, Jan. *Altnordisches Etymologisches Worterbuch.* Leiden: Brill, 1959.

Evans, David A. H., ed. *Hávamál.* London: Viking Society for Northern Research, 1986.

Evans, David A. H. and Faulkes, Anthony. *Hávamál: Glossary and Index.* London: Viking Society for Northern Research, 1987.

Grundy, Stephan. *Miscellaneous Studies towards the Cult of Óðinn.* New Haven, Conn.: The Troth, 2014.

Liberman, Anatoly. *An Analytic Dictionary of English Etymology: An Introduction.* Minneapolis: University of Minnesota Press, 2008.

McKinnell, John. "The Evolution of *Hávamál.*" *Essays on Eddic Poetry* (ed. Donata Kick and John D. Shafer). Pp. 59-95. Toronto: University of Toronto Press, 2014.

Saxo Grammaticus (transl. Peter Fisher, ed. Hilda Ellis Davidson). *History of the Danes, Books I–IX.*

Snorri Sturluson (ed. Anthony Faulkes). *Edda.* Vol. 1: *Prologue and Gylfaginning.* Vol. 2a: *Skaldskaparmál: Introduction, Text, and Notes.* Vol. 2b: *Skáldskaparmál: Glossary and Index of Names.* London: Viking Society for Northern Research, 2005-2008.

— (transl. Anthony Faulkes). *Edda.* London: J. M. Dent 1987.

Tacitus (ed. Maurice Hutton). *Dialogus; Agricola; Germania.* Loeb Classical Library. Cambridge, Mass.: Harvard University Press, 1914.

Wechsler, Robert. *Performing Without a Stage: The Art of Literary Translation.* North Haven, Conn.: Catbird Press, 1998.

ENDNOTES

1. See McKinnell, "The Evolution of *Hávamál*", for a full discussion of the poem's probable origins.

2. Wechsler, *Performing Without A Stage*, discusses the link between translation and performance.

3. The meaning of this phrase turns on the meaning of *brandr*. *Brandr* often means "firebrand; burning piece of wood". In the plural, it can mean "hearth fire", but could also be "logpile; wood pieces meant for burning." *Brandr* is also a poetic term for "sword". Different translators have disagreed over the meaning; it's not quite clear whether the guest is on the logpile (Dronke), on the threshhold (Crawford), by the fire (Bray, Chisholm, Dodds, Hollander, Larrington, Orchard, Taylor), or wielding swords (Bellows). I've followed Dronke here; someone who has to sit outside on the logpile, in the cold, would be impatient to come inside and try to gain acceptance.

4. *Endrþaga*, translated as "silence in turn", is a compound of *endr*, "again"—often corresponding to the English prefix "re"—and *þaga*, "silence". Bray, Chisholm, and Hollander read this word as *endrþega*, which would mean "acceptance again"; i.e. being invited again.

5. This is a tricky verse (Evans, p. 79), but the sense seems to be that a man is lucky to get outward praise, but he may find it harder to deal with what people really think of him.

6. Similar advice appears in the Old English poem *The Gifts of Men*: *Sum bið wonspedig, heardsælig hæle, bið hwæþre gleaw modes cræfta.* "One man is poor, a man with hard luck, yet he is skilled in mind-craft."

7. *Veit til sins geðs* literally means "he knows his own mind", but

almost the same expression is used in verse 20, and the sense seems to be "controls himself."

8. Hollander suggests that the "heron of forgetfulness" (*óminnishegri*) refers to magical or shamanic use of the heron's feathers. It's also been suggested that the "heron" is a bird-shaped ladle used to serve the ale. But there may be a more mundane reason for associating herons with drunkenness: herons vomit when they're disturbed. German still has the expression *kotzen wie ein Reiher*, "to puke like a heron" (the English equivalent would be "to be as sick as a dog").

9. *Gunnlöð* is the giantess from whom Odin steals the mead of inspiration; the story is told in verses 104 to 110, and in Snorri Sturluson's *Edda* (*Skáldskaparmál* ch. G57; ed. Faulkes, pp. 3-5; transl. Faulkes, *Edda*, pp. 61-64).

10. *Fjalarr* is one of the dwarves that brewed the mead of inspiration from the blood of the wise Kvasir. The known mythology does not record any visit by Odin to Fjalar; the story of the winning of the mead has it that Fjalar and his brother Galar hoard the mead until it is taken by the giant Suttung, and Odin has to steal it from Suttung and his daughter Gunnlöd. It is possible that the Fjalar named in this verse is a different being.

11. Translators differ over how to render the last line. Some editions of the text give the last line as a complete sentence: *Sá er vitandi vits*, "He is knowing of wit", i.e. "He's got good sense," which Crawford, Dodds, Dronke, Orchard, and I follow. But the *Codex Regius* makes this into a relative clause: *sá er vitandi er vits*, "he who is knowing of wit". In this case the "he" could be the wide-travelling man in line 1 (Chisholm, Hollander, Larrington) or "every man" in line 5 (Bellows, Bray).

12. Some translators (Bellows, Chisholm, Hollander) interpret *halda* as meaning "hold back from" and read the line as "A man shouldn't refuse the cup." But the line probably refers to the custom of passing around a common drinking vessel. Then *halda* would have the sense of "hang onto; cling to", and the line would mean "Don't refuse to pass around the

cup," i.e. "Don't hog all the booze."

13. Or possibly "what happens to a man."

14. *Þurrfjallr*, "dry-skinned," is a metaphor; the idea is that the man avoids being "showered" with ridicule by not being exposed as a fool. A similar English idiom would be "he dodges a bullet".

15. Translators differ over whether the person who escapes is the guest who mocks (Bellows, Bray, Dronke, Orchard), or the mocked guest (Crawford, Hollander), or someone else on the scene, possibly a bystander who just wants to get out of the way before a fight starts (Chisholm, Dodds, Larrington, Terry, this translation).

16. The *Codex Regius* seems to be missing a word; it just has *síns féar svági*, "of his own wealth, so not. . . ". The sense is clearly "so generous with his own wealth". Faulkes and Foote suggest that *svági* is a mistake for *svá gjöflan*, "so generous."

17. The line *þat er á sjalfum sýnst* is sometimes translated something like "one knows this best from one's own experience" (e.g. Bellows, Bray) or "that is obvious; that shows" (Crawford, Larrington, Orchard). But the more literal translation "that may be seen on themselves" seems more accurate—i.e., friends openly wear the fine clothes and weapons that they have given each other.

18. The last line, *maðr er manns gaman*, also turns up in the "Old Icelandic Rune Poem", in the M-rune verse. Whether the Rune Poem borrowed the line from *Hávamál*, or whether they both go back to a common source, I do not know.

19. The last line has been translated various ways; the stingy man is either greedy to get gifts (Auden, Chisholm); or unwilling to give gifts (Bellows, Bray, Hollander); or uncomfortable with receiving gifts, probably because he will have to give something in exchange (Dodds, Dronke, Larrington). Of course, he could be all of these at once.

20. The word *trémaðr* is a compound of *tré*, "tree; wood" + *maðr*, "man". Crawford and Terry translate this as "scarecrows", Bray as "landmarks", and Dodds as "wooden men". But in *Ragnars saga* and in an episode in *Flateyjarbók*, this word clearly

means a wooden idol that receives sacrifices. In another *Flateyjarbók* episode, it means a wooden statue made for sorcery.

21. The word *þorp* usually means "farmstead" in Norse, and Crawford translates it this way. Most translators render it as "hill; hillside" (Bellows, Bray, Larrington), "grove" (Dodds), or "field; bare ground" (Chisholm, Dronke, Hollander, Terry). However, (1) the evidence that *þorp* ever had these meanings is thin; and (2) fir trees actually grow well on hills and in bare ground. Evans (*Hávamál*, pp. 95-97) suggests that a fir tree on a farm would be constantly nibbled at by livestock, and possibly have people stripping its branches and bark. Instead of an image of a tree growing all alone, we have a tree struggling to survive being nibbled to death, in a place where no one is tending it.

22. The phrase *með höllu keri* means "with a tilted cup". I like Anne Holtsmark's interpretation that this refers to a man sharing a simple meal; he cuts his bread in half and pours half of his drink into the other's cup.

23. *Félaga* in the last line could refer to either one or several comrades; most translators assume it's one comrade, but Bray and Terry render it as plural.

24. This puzzling verse is probably corrupt, so that we may never know the exact original meaning. The genitives *Lítilla sanda* and *lítilla sæva* could be "genitives of place", meaning "on little sands, on little seas" (Dodds, Orchard), or "on the little sands of little seas" (Dronke). Dronke interprets the whole as "the minds of men [who live on] the little sands of little lakes [i.e. who never get out and see the world] are small." The last line is also unclear; translators have had to guess to make this verse make sense.

25. As the verse stands, the last half seems to contradict the first half. The first half warns against being too wise, and then the second half says that those who are wise live best. Some scholars think that a negative was accidentally omitted from the text we have—perhaps *er* ("it is") should be *erat* ("it is not") in the third line (Bray, Orchard, Terry). The word *vel*

might also means, not exactly "well", but "just enough", "just the right amount"; Crawford, Dodds, Hollander, Larrington, and I have taken that suggestion.

26. The word *dul* can mean "concealment", "silence", "stupidity", and/or "conceit". Most translators render this as "silence", but several verses praise keeping silent. I chose "being conceited", thinking that there's a difference between keeping quiet in order to listen and learn, and refusing to participate in a conversation because you're too stupid and/ or too conceited, which seems to be what *dul* implies here.

27. Saxo Grammaticus quotes this verse (translated into Latin) in his *Danish History*, as a saying of Erik the Eloquent, a legendary king of Norway: "Whoever intends to scale another's pinnacle must be watchful and wakeful. Nobody has ever won victory by snoring, nor has any sleeping wolf found a carcase." (V.155; transl. Fisher, p. 145)

28. The second half of this verse is tricky to translate, although the general sense seems clear. The word *né*, "not", could possibly mean "neither/nor"; the sense would be "Neither one man nor another must know". It's also not clear whether *einn*, "one [man]", is meant to be the person addressed in the verse, who shouldn't tell anyone at all his secret (Chisholm), or instead, the one person that the secret-keeper may confide in (Bellows, Crawford, Bray, Hollander).

29. The *Codex Regius* only contains the last two lines. Later paper manuscripts add the first two lines, but only Bray and Hollander have translated them.

30. Auden, Bellows, Bray, Chisholm, and Hollander assume that the payback for words is a bad thing. But this is not necessarily what the original means; the payback for speech could presumably be good or bad.

31. There's been some question over what the last word should be. *lið* with a long *i* is a poetic word for ale or cider, and the sense might be "a hated man seldom gets a drink" (Crawford, Terry). Chisholm translates this line as "among the folk", reading the word as *lið* with a short *i*, meaning "folk, people; troops, army". But most scholars read the word as

liðr, meaning a joint or a limb. The metaphor, still in use in Icelandic, refers to butchering an animal: "to find the joint", i.e. to find the natural place to cut up a carcass, means "to do something at just the right time."

32. *Hengi* could be the subjunctive of either *hanga*, "to be hanging", or *hengja* "to hang [something]", so the line could read "if two hams were to hang" (Bray, Dodds, Dronke, Larrington, Orchard, Terry) or "if I were to hang up two hams" (Bellows, Chisholm, Crawford, Hollander). I follow the interpretation that the guest is expected to pay his host back double the value of what he's consumed; "true friend" would be meant ironically. But Dronke reads it unironically: my friend has two hams hanging, so plenty of food to offer me, but I've already eaten. Auden also reads it unironically; my hosts treat me as if I've already eaten a ham with a friend who had two hanging up.

33. *illa heill* can mean either "poor fortune, bad luck" (Dronke, Larrington) or "ill health" (Auden, Bellows, Bray, Chisholm, Crawford, Dodds, Hollander, Orchard, Terry).

34. Most translators assume that *vel* in the last line an adjective applying to *verkum*, making the line mean "one [is blessed] by good deeds," but this is grammatically questionable. Faulkes suggests that *vel* modifies the adjective *sæll*, "blessed", in line 3. I've followed this suggestion here, as did Dronke and Orchard.

35. The question here is whether *dauðr*, "dead [man]", refers to the wealthy man in the preceding line, or to someone else. Bellows, Bray, Crawford, Dodds, Dronke, Larrington, and Orchard interpret this verse to mean that the wealthy man himself is dead. Auden, Chisholm, Hollander, and Terry assume that the wealthy man is alive and enjoying his fire, while the dead man is out in the cold. This interpretation seems to fit the first half of the line best, and also fit verse 71 in emphasizing the contrast between being alive and being dead. Evans suggests that *dauðr* could mean death itself (usually *dauði*). The sense would then be "I saw the rich man enjoying his fire, but death was at his door."

36. Evans's commentary cites differing opinions as to what lines 1-3 are getting at. What makes the most sense to me is this: Viking-era ships usually put into shore at night, and one who could trust that he had enough food would be glad, because he would soon be able to get off the boat, cook a hot meal, and sleep well. On coastal voyages, ships had to navigate rocks and narrow fjords, and the wind could blow up quickly; under those conditions, the yardarms of a ship had to be short, because a ship with too large a sail would be harder to steer safely. The word *ráar* in line 3, "yardarms", could also mean "corners", and Bray, Chisholm, Hollander, and Terry interpret it to mean sleeping quarters aboard a ship, but Faulkes doubts this interpretation.

37. Larrington and Orchard leave out the negative at the start of the verse, changing the sense to "even a man who knows nothing, knows that. . ."

38. The name Fitjung might come from the same root as "fat" (*feitr*), so that Fitjung would mean "Fatty". Bray follows this interpretation. Faulkes suggests that it may come from a word meaning "lowland meadows"—i.e. the place where Fitjung has his farm. The name may have been chosen only to alliterate, and have no other significance.

39. The line could be read as either "what you ask the runes" or " when you ask the runes". Dodds, Chisholm, and Hollander translate it "when"; the others either read "what" or rework the line completely.

40. The word translated "known by the Advisors" is *reginkunnr*. *Kunnr* normally means "known", but in some instances the sense is clearly "descended from" (Evans, *Hávamál*, p. 114). Chisholm, Dodds, and Hollander imply "known"; Bellows, Bray, Dronke, and Orchard imply "descended." The word *reginkunnr* definitely goes back to pre-Christian times, appearing on the 7th-century Noleby stone: **runo fahi reginkundu**, "Runes I color, descended from the Advisors". It also appears on the 9th-century Sparlosa stone: **rað runaʀ þaʀ ræginkundu**, "interpret the runes there, descended from the Advisors".

41. It would take a sizable essay to unpack exactly what terms like *ginnregin* and *fimbulþulr* mean. The prefix *ginn-*, as in *Ginnungagap*, can mean "great; vast" (compare Old English *gin*, *ginn*, meaning "a wide expanse"), but Cleasby and Vigfusson relate it to Modern English *begin*, *beginning*. *Regin* is a poetic word for the gods; Jan de Vries interprets it as "the Advisors" (*die Beratenden*), linking it with Gothic *ragin*, "counsel, decision", and connecting it ultimately with a root meaning "speak; say; pronounce" (*Altnordisches Etymologisches Wörterbuch*, vol. 7, pp. 436-437). *Þulr* is related to *þylja*, "to mutter, to chant, to recite", and *þula*, a type of poetic list of names; the Old English cognate *þyle* is glossed in Latin as *orator*. I went with "Speaker" here.

42. Some translators assume that the "you" in line 2 is the same person as the "he" in line 6 (Crawford, Dodds, Terry). One commentator interpreted "he" in line 6 to be referring to the mighty thul (presumably Odin) in line 5: in other words, if you ask of the runes, it's best if Odin doesn't tell you anything. (Evans, *Hávamál*, p. 114)

43. "A woman when burned" refers to her funeral pyre; the sense is that a woman cannot be said to be truly praiseworthy until her life is over. Chisholm and Hollander translates the line as "a torch when burned", seemingly amending *konu* to *kén*, which doesn't exist in the standard dictionaries but which looks like Old English *cén*, "torch". However, the text seems clear enough as it stands.

44. Ice skates were made from cow metatarsal bones, which have a naturally flat side for the foot and a keeled side to glide over the ice. These bones required minimal carving to make functional skates. Such skates have been found in archaeological sites all over northern Europe, and stayed in use in some areas until the early 1900s.

45. The verse contrasts feeding your horse *heima*, "at [your] home," and feeding the dog *á búi*, which probably means "at someone else's home". The idea may be that you should fatten your own horse, but let your dog scrounge on whatever he can scavenge from your neighbors. (Evans, *Hávamál*, p. 115)

The translator has observed that this is a common method of dog-raising in the rural United States to this day.

46. *hverfandi hvél* is given in *Álvissmál* as a name for the moon, and it's been suggested that the sense here is that women's hearts are as changeable as the moon. But there may also be some influence from the widespread medieval idea of Fortune and her wheel; this definitely turns up in later Norse texts.

47. In several saga episodes, the cawing of a crow or raven is taken as an omen (Evans, *Hávamál*, p. 116)

48. Evans suggests that the phrase *fallanda báru* has the technical meaning of a wave breaking on a submerged rock—obviously a treacherous situation for sailors.

49. There are instances in the sagas of a seeress who can be bribed to give the prophecies that someone wants to hear; see, for example, *Hrólfs saga kraka* ch. 3.

50. Verses 85-89 are clearly a connected sequence. Several translators (Auden, Bellows, Crawford, Hollander, Terry) switch verses 88 and 89, as 88 seems to break the flow.

51. The pithy last line *sá fær, er fríar* is often expanded quite a bit in translations; Dronke's "He wins who woos" is probably the best that can be done.

52. *Billings mey* means "Billing's girl", and it's not clear whether she is his wife or daughter. I have followed Evans (p. 120) in assuming that she is his wife, which fits verse 102 better.

53. The text is clear that the dog is not merely tethered to the bed, but has been tied *onto* the bed, because the girl is mockingly inviting Odin to have sex with it. (Evans, p. 119)

54. At this point Odin begins telling how he won the mead *Óðrerir*, "inspiration-stirrer", from the giant Suttung, by seducing Suttung's daughter Gunnlod. The myth is told in full in Snorri Sturluson's *Edda* (*Skáldskaparmál* ch. G57, ed. Faulkes, pp. 3-5; transl. Faulkes, pp. 61-64.)

55. *Rati*, "traveler", is the name of the auger that Odin uses to bore into Gunnlod's chamber in the form of a snake.

56. The phrase *vel keypts litar* literally means "well-bought appearance" and is often assumed to be corrupt. Bellows and Larrington render it as "beauty", referring to Gunnlod

herself; others emend *litar* to *hlutar*, "of the portion; of the share". However, shapeshifters are sometimes said to change their own *lit*, and I interpret the line as referring to Odin's ability to shapeshift. Bray, Dodds, and Orchard have done something similar.

57. The line *á alda vés jarðar* is probably corrupt; it is often emended to *á alda vés jaðar*, "to the rim of the sacred place of men." But *jaðarr* can also mean "protector; lord", and I've followed this here. See the discussion in Evans, pp. 121-122.

58. *Bölverk*, "Evil Deed", is one of Odin's names; according to Snorri, it is the name that Odin used when he went to win the mead of poetry. The point seems to be that the giants don't even realize that Hár (the High One) and Bölverk are the same.

59. *Loddfáfnir* was interpreted as "Stray-Singer" by Bray, but *lodd-* seems to mean "ragtag; worthless fellow" (related to *loð-*, "shaggy", *lydda*, "rogue, scoundrel", and *lodda*, "whore"; possibly also German *verlottert*, "run-down; lazy"), while *Fáfnir* is the name of the most famous dragon in Norse mythology, the one slain by Sigurd. (I was tempted to translate it "Ragdragon".) Liberman suggests that the name may be part of an initiation rite, in which an unproven, worthless youth with an insulting name is given wisdom and becomes a warrior and hero. (*Analytic Dictionary*, p. 138-140)

60. The wife is literally said to be an *eyrarúna*, literally "ear-rune", but meaning a confidant, someone who whispers secrets into your ear or vice versa.

61. *Gamanrúnar* is literally "runes of joy", but is usually translated as "cheerful speech", "intimacy", "trust", or "friendship". Auden, Dronke, and Hollander assume that *liknargaldr*, literally "healing spell", is also metaphorical. I've chosen to imply that magic might be afoot, especially in the light of Odin's later boast of knowing magic spells that can soothe enmity (153) and heal (147).

62. An abbreviated word in the manuscript means that this line could be read in two ways: "say that that is evil", i.e. call it what it is (Auden, Bellows, Chisholm, Crawford, Dodds,

Larrington, Orchard) or "say that it is evil for yourself", i.e., when you see evil, regard it as harmful to you (Bray, Hollander, Terry).

63. The mouths of old men are humorously called shriveled bags. Most translators seem to assume that the fact that the bags are hanging up among hides and skins is just an extension of the metaphor. However, Rolf Pipping (cited in Evans, p. 129) suggested that the "grey-haired speaker" (*þulr*) who gives sensible advice is a shaman or magician imitating Odin himself, who won knowledge through hanging on the World Tree (verses 138-139; see also 157). Some accounts of sacrifices describe multiple human and animal victims hanged from a tree (e.g. Adam of Bremen, *History of the Archbishops* IV.27, transl. Tschan, p. 208). A sacrificed man (or god) might well be thought of as hanging among the withered remains of earlier sacrifices.

64. This verse has puzzled some scholars, because the first two lines imply "don't be too hospitable" and the second imply "be generous to everyone". Hollander interpreted *baugr*, "ring", as "anus", and translated "give a ring" as "show the beggar your back" (i.e. "your behind"). Bellows suggests that the ring is a door-ring that you must give the door-beam, or else the beam will cause you trouble; in other words, you must sometimes latch your door, or else excess hospitality will be your downfall. The contradiction may not be real; both verses suggest that you must be hospitable, so you'd better make sure you have the resources to give what hospitality demands.

65. The bracketed lines are generally thought to have been added later, and include "home remedies" that are attested in later manuscripts and folk practices. There are difficulties with the text, and translators have disagreed much about how to render it.

66. According to Snorri Sturluson's *Edda*, Bestla is Odin's mother (*Gylfaginning* 6, ed. Faulkes, p. 11; transl. Faulkes, *Edda*, p. 11).

67. *ausinn Óðreri* is usually taken to refer the mead sprinkled or poured from Odroerir, if Odroerir is the cauldron that

contains the mead, as Snorri's *Edda* states. However, in this poem Odroerir seems to refer only to the mead itself. Bray and Dronke suggest that it is Odin himself who is sprinkled with the mead Odroerir.

68. *Þundr* is a name of Odin; it may mean "Rumbler" (Grundy, *Miscellaneous Studies*, p. 82).

69. This refers to cursing enemies by carving runes on wood, as attested in *Grettis saga* ch. 79. The line is unclear as written, and has been emended to "on roots of a sapling / sappy wood" (Auden, Bellows, Bray, Chisholm, Larrington) or "on the roots of a gnarled tree" (Hollander). The emendation "on the roots of a strong tree" is suggested by Evans (*Hávamál*, pp. 138-139) and followed by Dodds and Orchard.

70. *Túnriður*, "hedge-riders" or "fence-riders", are shapeshifting witches of some sort, who could send their spirits out in animal form while their bodies remained behind. See Evans, *Hávamál*, pp. 139-141.

71. The verb *gala*, "chant", could also be translated as "howl". Tacitus reports that Germanic warriors went into battle shouting war-cries called *barritus*, placing their shields beside their mouths to deepen the tone. (*Germania* 3, transl. Hutton, pp. 266-269)

72. This probably refers to the pre-Christian rite of sprinkling newborn babies with water, which was practiced in pre-Christian times.

73. *Dellingr* is listed in Snorri's *Edda* as one of the Æsir gods, the third husband of the giantess *Nótt* (Night) and father of Dagr (Day) (*Gylfaginning* 10; ed. Faulkes, p. 13; transl. Faulkes, *Edda*, pp. 13-14). *Hroptatýr* is a name of Odin; it could be related to Norse *hrópa*, meaning both "to cry out" and "to slander". *Hroptatýr* could mean either "the slandered god" or "the god who cries out", but its meaning is still considered obscure (de Vries, *Altnordische Etymologisches Worterbuch*, vol. 5, p. 260; Grundy, *Miscellaneous Studies*, p. 74).